Words of Wisdom

Compiled by Mark Ziaian

Published, 2020, by Transmedia Translating and Publishing Co., a branch of Intermedia Educational Co. Ltd, 2701-2 Forest Laneway, Toronto, Ontario, M2N 5X7. Phone: 1 647 454 0220. Email: intermediaeducational@gmail.com

Printed and distributed by Kindle Direct Publishing, Amazon

Ziaian, Mark (compiled by)
Words of Wisdom, Volume 1, 100 p + Index
Copyright 2020 Internationalmark
ISBN 978-1-896574-03-5

1. Quotes. 2. Proverbs. 3. Sayings. 1. Title

Cover: Mark Ziaian

I would like to thank everyone who sent in quotes to my interactive pages at www.internationalmark.co.uk

After almost two decades, I decided to take the quotes down and make them available in paperback.

All the quotes in this book are from my website sent in by members of the public and are by famous, infamous or even unknown people who wanted to share something with the world. Most of the sayings by unknown people cannot be found in any other publication.

I have tried to make as few changes as possible and publish what was originally sent to me. For this reason, some of the quotes will remain uncredited. Thus, the book is called "Words of Wisdom" and not "The Book of Quotes".

For practicallty, *Words of Wisdom* will be published in two volumes. This is Volume 1.

Mark Ziaian

Words of Wisdom

"There is happiness in little things
There is joy in passing pleasure
But friendship is from year to year
The best of all life's treasure"

*****

"Earth provides enough to satisfy every man's needs,
but not every man's greed." - Mahatma Gandhi

*****

"Love makes the world go round
Hate puts you in the ground" - Mark Ziaian

*****

"Whether you think you can, or you think you cannot,
you are right." - Henry Ford

*****

"Don't bring a knife to a gun fight."

*****

"Our task must be to free ourselves by widening our
circle of compassion to embrace all living creatures
and the whole of nature and its beauty."
- Albert Einstein

*****

"Do, or do not, there is no try."
- Yoda (Empire Strikes Back)

*****

"Why ask why not, but why not ask why?"

*****

"Love is a game, there are the winners and the losers. The losers don't know they are playing and the winners do, but it takes two to play a game."

*****

"Searching for someone else to blame.
Hoping I won't go insane.
Selfish pride my only gain.
Faking Sanity." - Five Iron Frenzy

*****

"Life is not always fair, deal with it."

*****

"Great spirits have always encountered violent opposition from mediocre minds." - Albert Einstein

*****

"Things don't change. We change."
- Henry David Thoreau

*****

"Those who are sad now will be happy, because God will comfort them. Those who want to do right more than anything else are happy, because God will fully satisfy them." - Matthew 5:4,6

*****

"A dog that barks a lot is never a good hunter"

*****

"Faith is the only thing some men possess and is the only thing all men should possess."

*****

"Life is merely a play being acted out while simultaneously written by its performers."

*****

"No pain, no gain."

*****

"Man's worst enemy is himself."

*****

"To learn from a mistake, you must first admit that you have made one."

*****

"You can run from the devil but, you can't run from God."

*****

"Laughter is the physical form of happiness."

*****

 "You can do whatever you want to do in this world, just don't get caught."

*****

"Life sucks; kill yourself or get over it."

*****

"There will always be another time, place or person."

*****

"The only thing standing between me and greatness is me." - Woody Allen

*****

"What is truly amazing is when gold dust is turned to silver."

*****

"Lead from the back, and let others believe they are in front." - Nelson Mandela

*****

"When things look bad, close your eyes."

*****

"When someone asks you how you are, and your reply is "bad", you are being selfish, for there are many that are much worse off than you."

*****

"There are better times to come, but first you must survive the worst."

*****

"The people who see a murderer and, instead of feeling hate toward them, feel sorrow and pain, are the people who understand life itself."

*****

"To people who sit back and watch saying 'that seems easy' … lie."

*****

"To will oneself to go on, even when they feel they can't, is true strength."

*****

"Love is just a word composed of 4 letters, that someone made up to try to express feelings too great for words."

*****

"Dreams are a distorted vision composed through the heart."

*****

"Life is what happens to you while you're busy making other plans." - Allen Saunders

*****

"Words hurt more than sticks and stones
It hurts when it's my heart instead of my bones
I can count on you to be true
When I am hurt I can run to you."

*****

"However difficult life may seem, there is always something you can do and succeed at."
- Stephen Hawking

*****

"We are what we do repeatedly. Excellence then is not an act, but a habit." - Will Durant

*****

"The true measure of a man is not by what he has done or what he will do, but what he has had the power to do."

*****

"Pick a job you like, and you will never have to work a day of your life."

*****

"Loving someone who does not know is better than telling them and being rejected for life. For there is always hope that they too, love you." - Made by anonymous while reading all other quotes.

*****

"Don't tell anybody everything you know."

*****

"When you are angry, you are hurt."

*****

"Young people nowadays assume that money is everything, and when they get older, they know it."
- Oscar Wilde

*****

"Fifty percent of all weasel deaths is caused by parts in reclining chairs."

*****

"Never flush the toilet while taking a shower."

*****

"Power brings corruption and corruption feeds on power."

*****

"It is better to be silent and be thought a fool than to speak out and remove all doubt." - Mark Twain

*****

"A jack of all trades is a merchant of none."

*****

"Come on Eileen, I swear that Eileen, at this moment you mean everything to me, too rah loo rah ay."

*****

"A real man is he who finds salvation in a woman."

*****

"The best way to predict the future is to create it."

*****

"A bend in the road is not the end of the road .... unless you fail to make the turn."

*****

"Don't ask me to be kind; just ask me to behave as if I were." - Jules Renard

*****

"Never over-estimate the intelligence of other people."

*****

"Better to have loved and lost than to have never loved at all." - Alfred Lord Tennyson

*****

"A sad thing in life is when you meet someone who means a lot to you, only to find out in the end that it was never meant to be, and you just have to let "it" go."

*****

"The feet you step on today may be connected to the a**e you kiss tomorrow."

*****

"Need a penny take a penny. Need two pennies get a job."

*****

"What is meant to be shall be. So don't stress, God can handle it."

*****

"Tip 15% or stay home!" - wise waiter

*****

"Dream your fantasy, but act on reality"

*****

"When the tide comes in all boats rise."

*****

"Sex is like math: add the bed...subtract the clothes...divide the legs.... and hope you don't multiply."

*****

"Don't hate because of looks, only bestow hate on people for the way they act."

*****

"People who have money think that they are better, people with out as much money know they are better."

*****

"Never pick a fight with ugly people, they have nothing to lose." - Robin Williams

*****

"There is no gravity, the world just sucks."

*****

"Madness takes its toll, please have the exact change."

*****

"Death is only the beginning of something new."

*****

"It is better to be hated for who you are than to be loved for who you're not." - Bette Davis

*****

"Mess with the best, die like the rest" - Hackers

*****

"Friends are only friends when they have proven themselves true, but to make your friends prove true, you should prove true too."

*****

"You always remember the first."

*****

"What is the difference between infatuation and love?"

*****

"In a super model world, I have begun to feel very much like a runway." - Becky Weisberg

*****

"Into paradise may the angels lead you."

*****

"If it's stupid but works, it isn't stupid."

*****

"There is more to life than who we are."

*****

"He who is in love with himself has at least this advantage - he won't encounter many rivals."
- Georg Christoph Lichtenberg

*****

"Forget about yesterday because it is the past, live for today because it is the present, and think about tomorrow because it is your future."

*****

"Never look down on someone unless you're helping him/her up." - Jesse Jackson

*****

"Live every day of your life like it would be your last, because you start dying as soon as you're born."

*****

"Enjoy what you have now, because it won't be there forever."

*****

"I refuse to join a club that would have me for a member." - Groucho Marx

*****

"Anyone who says sunshine brings happiness, has never danced in the rain."

*****

"Life is a game. Those who choose to ignore the game are truly living, though those who play the game are dying."

*****

"In love we often doubt what we most believe."

*****

"You must love yourself before you can love anyone else."

*****

"Never frown because you never know who is falling in love with your smile."

*****

"If you want your dreams to come true then don't sleep." -Yiddish Proverb

*****

"Shorter a breath one day closer to death."
- Pink Floyd

*****

"I went on a walk to Greenwich, on my way seeing a coffin with a dead body in it, dead of plague. This disease makes us more cruel to one another than we are to dogs." - Samuel Pepys 22nd August 1665.

*****

"Never deny yourself love because someone tells you to. Deny love because you haven't found it yet."

*****

"Ninety-eight percent of the adults in this country are decent, hard-working honest Americans. It's the other lousy two percent that get all the publicity. But then, we elected them." - Lily Tomlin

*****

"Anything worth having is worth waiting for."

*****

"To be patriotic, hate all nations but your own; to be religious, all sects but your own; to be moral, all pretences but your own." - Lionel Strachey

*****

"Everybody has dreams, life just has a way of making you forget what they are." - Wild America

*****

"Real friends stab you in the front."

*****

"Marriage is a wonderful institution, but who wants to live in an institution?" - Groucho Marx

*****

"Just remember, if the world didn't suck... we would all fall off."

*****

"Unlock yourself and step out of your box. Raise the sails and leave the harbour. It is the only way to see the vastness of the ocean that we call emotions."

*****

"He who kneels before God can stand before anyone."

*****

"We walk by faith not by sight."

*****

"If you can't be a good example, then you'll just have to be a horrible warning."
- Catherine Aird

*****

"If at first you don't succeed, f*** the world then smoke the weed."

*****

"To win a war is as disastrous as to lose."
- Agatha Christie

*****

"Human nature is deeply and permanently flawed, and we can do nothing with or for the human race until we recognize its moral and intellectual limitations."
- Jonathan Swift

*****

"Such is life" - Ned Kelly

*****

"In honour I gain them and in honour I die with them."

*****

"Don't pass through the gates of life unnoticed."

*****

"Even in ignorance there is some Wisdom."

*****

"Time heals what reason cannot."
- Seneca the Younger

*****

"Nobody can make you feel inferior without your consent." - Elanor Roosevelt

*****

"Yesterday is history, tomorrow is a mystery, today is a gift. That's why they call it the present." - Bill Keane

*****

"Enjoy life. There's plenty of time to be dead."

*****

"To those who think God is a swear word, if we are to blame God for everything that goes wrong, we must also thank him for everything that goes right."

*****

"Man is not a rational animal but merely an animal capable of reason."

*****

"Don't sweat the petty things, and don't pet the sweaty things." - Mark Lewis.

*****

"Duct tape is like the force: It had a light side and a dark side, and it holds the universe together."
- Carl Zwanzig

*****

"Don't you know what's out there in the world? Princes, yes, but wolves and humans too."

*****

"Ninety percent of the politicians give the other ten percent a bad name." - Henry Kissinger

*****

"I like the pope, the pope smokes dope."

*****

"Faith is the substance of things hoped for, the evidence of things not seen."
- Hebrews 11, new King James version

*****

"And in the end the love that you take will all equal up to the love that you make." -The Beatles

*****

"Those who think that they know too much, only know that they know too little."

*****

"Some cause happiness wherever they go; others, whenever they go." - Oscar Wilde

*****

"Every man dies, but not every man really lives."
- Brave Heart

*****

"You know it's love when you lay awake in bed at night with a smile on your face because you know that the reality beats any dream you could imagine."
- Katie

*****

"Whenever one person is found adequate to the discharge of a duty by close application thereto it is

worse when executed by two persons - and scarcely done at all if three or more are employed therein."
- George Washington

*****

"It's not your friends or advisors that make you stronger, it is your enemy for he is the one who trains, punishes, and eventually destroys you."

*****

"No man is better than any other man regardless of mental, physical or financial advantage. And the belief of superiority is ignorance."

*****

"It's better to have one angry person, than two."

*****

"People want what they can't have, once they have it they don't want it anymore."

*****

"Good Better Best, never let it rest until your good is better and your better best."

*****

"Life is a journey; you control your destination."

*****

"Hatred is formed by Jealousy. You hate me because I outsmart you, something you will never forgive me for. You may stop this individual, but you can't stop us all."

*****

"The God who gave us life, gave us liberty at the same time." - Thomas Jefferson

*****

"One touch of nature makes the whole world kin."
- William Shakespeare

*****

"Gays are people too."

*****

"Why are you telling me you don't love me when your heart obviously does?"

*****

"God in heaven, God above
Please protect the girl I love
Sent with a smile, sealed with a kiss
I love my girl who's reading this."

*****

"The devil we blame our atrocities on is really just each one of us, so don't expect the end of the world to come one day out of the blue, it's been happening every day for a long time." - Marilyn Manson

*****

"We are only pawns in a game, taking life one step at a time."

*****

"Think not what your country can do for you but what you can do for your country." - John F. Kennedy.

*****

"You don't have to close doors you don't have to."

*****

 "Life is the contrast between expectation and reality."

*****

"The world does not belong to man, man belongs to the world." - Ishmael

*****

"Truths that matter - important principles - are, in the final analysis, still only two or three. They are those that your mother taught you as a child." - Enzo Biagi

*****

"Question not who you are but who you were."

*****

"Be nice to your enemies, because it makes them so damn mad."

*****

"I see pain on the faces of humanity and I hope for their sake the world does end."

*****

"Some things are meant to be closed but your mind isn't one of them."

*****

"Why do people with closed minds always open their mouths?"

*****

"It takes a lifetime to build a good reputation but only a second to destroy one."

*****

"Love isn't a game, so don't play." - Julia Lynn Goebel

*****

"We are all just monkeys with clothes on."

*****

"Nobody will ever be there for you, so to get anywhere in life you should depend only on yourself."

*****

"Better watch the still water, rather than the vicious dog who drinks it."

*****

"There are gold ships and silver ships, but no ships are like friendships."

*****

"I hope you're hungry cuz you know where your dinner hangs." - A.J. Henderson

*****

"If I don't want to, I don't have to, and you can't make me."

*****

"You may have a friend and not be in love; but you can never have a love, who is not a friend."

*****

"You are you and I am I. If in the end we are together...it's beautiful."

*****

"Man is like a piece of cheese."

*****

"It's better to be gone and remembered than here and forgotten. Live life to the fullest."

*****

"Don't be sad when it's over, be happy it happened."

*****

"It'll be alright in the morning."

*****

"Fool me once shame on you, fool me twice shame on me."

*****

"If you love someone put their love in a circle instead of a heart, because hearts break but circles go on forever."

*****

"Why is it we all seek fame from our words to another, or even a feeling of comfort and duty?"

*****

"The best thing about the future is that it comes only one day at a time." - Abraham Lincoln

*****

"All I want is to be loved by another and yet my words fall in vain and I'll walk a lonely life, but I will never give up. Through pain and loss I will still keep the faith and watch the devil struggle to make me give up."

*****

"Fear is only a four-letter word."

*****

"We have come to this earth alone and shall leave alone."

*****

"Work like you don't need the money, love like you've never been hurt, dance like nobody's watching."

*****

"Keep your friends close but your enemies closer."
- The Godfather

*****

"Parts of life is like an Alabama road; it gets rougher and rougher."

*****

"The frame of my life is the real world."

*****

"Some people come into our lives and quickly go. Some stay for a while and leave footprints on our hearts, and we are never, ever the same."

*****

"For every evil under the sun
There is a remedy or there is none
If there be one seek till you find it

If there be none never mind it" - Mother Goose

*****

"We didn't lose the game; we just ran out of time."
-Vince Lombardi

*****

"Friends help you move. Real friends help you move dead bodies."

*****

"Everyone thinks of changing the world, yet no one thinks of changing himself." - Leo Tolstoy

*****

"Are you a proud soldier in God's army or just one of his secret agents?" - Martha Bolton

*****

"Some people haven't been rescued because they never yelled "help"." -Martha Bolton

*****

"Before I speak, I have something important to say."
- Groucho Marx

*****

"When you are in love with someone, you can't never find a reason why you love them. But once you find it, sooner or later you will find the reason that you want to leave them."

*****

"If I take care of my character, my reputation will take care of itself." - Dwight L. Moody

*****

"Kind words are the music of the world."
- Frederick William Faber

*****

"Don't be discouraged; everyone who got where he is started where he was." - Ralph Waldo Emerson

*****

"Little minds are tamed and subdued by misfortune, but great minds rise above them." - Charles Spurgeon

*****

"If you don't stand for something, you'll fall for anything." - Terence

*****

"He is my friend who speaks well behind my back."
- Thomas Fuller

*****

"A politician needs the ability to foretell what is going to happen tomorrow, next week, next month, and next year. And to have the ability afterwards to explain why it didn't happen." - Winston Churchill

*****

"Two can play at that game." - Dave Tsai

*****

"If someone does something bad to me, then I will do something twice as bad to them." -Dave Tsai

*****

"Everyone should try to be kind, and helpful all the time." - Dave Tsai "(pretty ironic, considering what my other two quotes are)."

*****

 "Why wait until Christmas or Thanksgiving to eat good."

*****

"A bat is only a rodent that can fly."

*****

"Even if a clock don't work it will be right twice a day."

*****

"Man is born free, and yet he is everywhere in chains." - Jean-Jacques Rousseau

*****

"A goal set, halfway reached." -Abraham Lincoln

*****

"Sometimes when we're waiting for God to speak, he's waiting for us to listen." - Martha Bolton

*****

"The best prophet of the future is the past."

*****

"Success isn't how far you've got, but the distance you travelled from where you started."

*****

"Don't look at yourself from others' eyes."

*****

"If the means are not right, the ends are not worth it." - Mahatma Gandhi

*****

"The game of Life is not so much as holding a good hand but playing a poor hand well."

*****

"Mr Smith, Sir, as an obvious outsider, what is your opinion of the human race?" - Staff Sergeant at The Royal Military Academy, Sandhurst

*****

"It is not the size of the dog in the fight, it is the size of the fight in the dog."

*****

"The only way to have a friend is to be one."
- Ralph Waldo Emerson

*****

"I like the dreams of the future better than the history of the pass." - Thomas Jefferson

*****

"Memories are treasures you should never let go."

- Danae Jacobson

*****

"True friendship multiplies the good in life and divides its evil." - Baltasar Gracian

*****

"Don't fall before you're pushed." - English Proverb

*****

"Ah, these diplomats, such chatterboxes. The only way to shut them up is to mow them down with a machine gun. Bulgaren, go get me one!"
- Joseph Stalin during a meeting with General Charles De Gaul.

*****

"Always be nice to people on the way up; because you'll meet the same people on the way down."
- Wilson Mizner

*****

"Be like a postage stamp. Stick to one thing until you get there." - Josh Billings

*****

"We are all inclined to judge ourselves by our ideals; others, by their acts." - Harold Nicolson

*****

"Shut up! Before I tell you to shut up."

*****

"You are in above your head."

*****

"Never say great words unless they are lead by an even better one."

*****

"I like you but we never see, you belong to me."

*****

"Destiny is a belief for those too weak to create their own."

*****

"You must believe in yourself before others can believe in you."

*****

"Beer, the cause, and solution, to all life's problems."
- Homer J Simpson

*****

"Don't try to be a great man, just be a man, and let history make its mind up."
- William T Riker - Star Trek TNG

*****

"The beatings will stop when morale improves."
- Japanese Submarine Commander - WW2

*****

"I am nervous as a longtail cat in a room full of rocking chairs."

*****

"Don't always look to the future, don't get stuck in the past, live for the moment but know it's not everything."

*****

"Remember me for Who I was not for what I shall become."

*****

"Instead of taking the right road, make your own and leave a trail."

*****

"If you haven't got anything to die for, you're not fit to be alive."

*****

"The way I see it, the more people that hate me, the less people I have to try to please."

*****

"I came, I saw, I conquered" - Julius Caesar

*****

"Alas the devil stood and felt how awful goodness is."

*****

"True love is found only when 2 people can share each other's solitude."

*****

"Friends listen to what you say, best friends listen to what you don't say."

*****

"Life is a game. only you don't play this game, it plays you."

*****

"All who wander are not lost."

*****

"I only laugh because it is funny."

*****

"Clowns, Clowns everywhere. Who gives a s**t what u care?"

*****

"People are people and dogs are dogs, cats are cats and that's that."

*****

"Don't be a nerd be a geek instead."

*****

"If you're missing your homework just tell the teacher/professor my computer ate it. You can never underestimate technology these days."

*****

"Don't teach a dog old tricks like rolling into cars or pi**ing on ice-cream."

*****

"My participation, my focus, my intensity, my sacrifice for my sport. This is who I am. It's not just something I do." - Jamila Wideman, WNBA

*****

"Sing a sweeter song the birds will follow you, sing a rotten song Slim Shady and Dr. Dre will admire you."

*****

"Man is incomplete until he is married. Then he is finished."

*****

"Chop your own wood, and it will warm you twice."
- Henry Ford

*****

"If you don't taste it, it's wasted." - Mark Ziaian

*****

"Open up your mind to all propositions that you encounter even if you don't always agree with them on this road we call life."

*****

"I don't like dogs because they think they are less than people, and I don't like cats because they think they are better than people, I like pigs because they are just the same as people." (told by some Hungarian)

*****

"If it does not say you cannot then you can."
- Philip Cotter

*****

"We shall not cease from exploration, and the end of all our exploring will be to arrive where we started and know the place for the first time." - T.S. Eliot

*****

"When elephants fight it is the grass that suffers."
- African proverb

*****

"Stop living in this negative way, make way for the positive day." - Bob Marley

*****

"If we do not maintain justice, justice will not maintain us." - Francis Bacon

*****

"It is easier for us to get to know God than to know our own soul. God is nearer to us than our soul, for He is the ground in which it stands...so if we want to know our own soul, and enjoy its fellowship, it is necessary to seek it in our Lord God."
- Julian of Norwich

*****

"I often quote myself. It adds spice to my conversation." - George Bernard Shaw

*****

"A lie gets halfway around the world before the truth has a chance to get its pants on." - Winston Churchill

*****

"I try to take one day at a time, but sometimes several days attack me at once." - Jennifer Unlimited

*****

"You cannot make someone love you. All you can do is be someone who can be loved."

*****

"The irony of looking for an easy way out is that most of the time it proves to be more difficult." - Griselda Chavez (I hope it's original. I thought of it as I was supposedly trying to peel garlic the easy way, which turned out to be the most difficult.)

*****

"Make everything as simple as possible, but not simpler." Albert Einstein

*****

"Don't lend money to your friends, you might lose them. Lend money to your enemies, you might lose them." - Mark Ziaian

*****

"You could be the world's best garbage man, the world's best model; it doesn't matter what you do if you're the best." - Muhammad Ali

*****

"Well done is better than well said."
- Benjamin Franklin

*****

"Just because you're winning it don't mean you're the lucky one."

*****

"Opportunity is missed by most people because it is dressed in overalls and looks like work." - Thomas Edison

*****

"The apple doesn't fall to go from the tree."

*****

"I don't want to achieve immortality through my work. I want to achieve it by not dying." - Woody Allen

*****

"A pessimist sees the difficulty in every opportunity; an optimist sees the opportunity in every difficulty."
- Sir Winston Churchill

*****

"Be unselfish: respect the selfishness of others."
- Stanislaw Jerzy Lec

*****

"Live, like there is no tomorrow."

*****

"Winning is not everything, but loosing is nothing."

*****

"Few wishes come true by themselves." - June Smith

*****

"The man who does not read good books has no advantage over the man who cannot read them."
- Mark Twain

*****

"Do you believe in rock and roll, can music save your mortal soul, will you teach me how to dance real slow?" - American Pie

*****

"We all commit certain acts in our lives on an unsavoury nature. Some bad, some worse, some unspeakable. Sometimes we suffer in silence. Sometimes we seek redemption. We get what we deserve, but the glowing light at the end of the tunnel may not be the beacon of righteousness that you are looking for. It might be the beginning of a disfigured life you only can dream of."

*****

"You can't build a reputation on what you are going to do." - Henry Ford

*****

"Too bad all the people who know how to run the country are busy driving taxi cabs and cutting hair."
- George Burns

*****

"A true friend stabs you in the front."

*****

"The more we know the better we forgive. Whoever feels deeply, feels for all who live." -Madame de Stael

*****

"Everything that can be invented has been invented."
- Charles H. Duel, Commissioner, U.S. Office of Patents

*****

"If you want to make God laugh, tell him about your plans." - Blaise Pascal

*****

"It is hard to be sincere if you are intelligent, in the same way as being honest when you are ambitious.
- Fernando Pessoa

*****

"I think there is a world market for maybe five computers."
- Thomas Watson, Chairman of IBM, 1943

*****

"We hope that, when the insects take over the world, they will remember with gratitude how we took them along on all our picnics." - Bill Vaughan

*****

"Think like a man of action. Act like a man of thought." - Henri Bergson

*****

"The true Sign of intelligence is not knowledge but imagination." - Albert Einstein

*****

"The better the friends you are with a boy/girl the better couple you would be."

*****

"Time wounds all heels." - Groucho Marx

*****

"When one door of happiness closes, another opens; but often we look so long at the closed door that we do not see the one which has opened for us."
- Helen Keller

*****

"My system? I have no system."
- Pierre Joseph Proudhon

*****

"Life is good, so why does everyone hate it?"

*****

"Life is a story that doesn't stop if you've given up all you could have learned and could have been."

*****

"All that's necessary for the forces of evil to win in the world is for enough good men to do nothing."
- Edmund Burke

*****

"Nothing is thicker than blood."

*****

"You don't love a woman because she is beautiful, but she is beautiful because you love her."

*****

"If a tree falls in the woods and nobody is there to hear it..., who the ***k cares!!"

*****

"I saw the best minds of my generation destroyed by madness." - Allen Ginsberg

*****

"Put three Englishmen on a deserted island and within an hour they'll have invented a class system."
- Sir Alan Ayckbourn, Playwright

*****

"If you weren't so busy staring in the mirror, I would tell you that you were beautiful."

*****

"I am a backseat driver; get out of my way I can't see around the head cushion."

*****

"Life throws a lot of s**t at us, so the best we can do is just grab it and do the best with it as we can."

*****

"Man cannot degrade women without himself falling into degradation, he cannot elevate her without at the same time elevating himself."- Alexander Walker

*****

"When it's dark enough, you can see the stars."
- Charles A. Beard

*****

"The Lord is my light and my salvation." - Ps.27 vs.1

*****

"Exalt the Lord our God and worship at his footstool. He is Holy." - Ps.99vs.5

*****

"Enjoy = Listen to the music in the words of silence."

*****

"I am a heavy burden on a person, I almost suffocate him and demand that he should carry me; and, without relieving him, I persuade myself and others that I am sorry and want to make it easy for him by all possible means, but not by allowing him to get rid of my weight." - Leo Tolstoy

*****

"When you love someone, always forgive the little things and work through the big things. This is the only way to love."

*****

"I'm drowning, so come inside, welcome to my filthy mind."

*****

"Life happens. Take it as it is without complaining or change your perspective."

*****

"Always keep your head held high, no matter what. No one can take away your pride unless you let them."

*****

"Friends are like four-leaf clovers hard to find, lucky to have."

*****

"If voting could really change things, it would be illegal."

*****

"Two men look out through the same bars: one sees the mud, and one sees the stars."
- Frederick Langbridge

*****

"Dream = Fly with your mind on the wings of illusion."

*****

"A mind all logic is like a knife all blade. It makes the hand bleed that uses it." - Rabindranath Tagore

*****

"A bank is a place that will lend you money if you can prove that you don't need it." - Bob Hope

*****

"It matters not whether you win or lose; what matters is whether I win or lose." - Darrin Weinberg

*****

"Fortune favours the brave."

*****

"Don't drink and drive! It might spill."

*****

"There is no use crying over spilled milk."

*****

"Life's a b***h and then you end up getting married to one, and the bitch ends up turning around and slapping you in the face."

*****

"Live hard, die young, and leave a good-looking corpse." - James Dean

*****

"Stoners live, stoners die, but down in hell, we still get high."

*****

"Military justice is to justice what military music is to music." - Groucho Marx

*****

"The production of too many useful things results in too many useless people." - Karl Marx

*****

"Seek respect rather than popularity, quality rather than luxury, refinement rather than fashion."

*****

"It takes only one person or one idea to change your life."

*****

"Don't play with fire, if you can't handle getting burnt."

*****

"Weapons are not bad, only the people who abuse them are bad."

*****

"Don't wear a pad in a pool."

*****

"Sex can wait, so masturbate."

*****

"The art of movement begins with a twirl."

*****

"You win some you lose some."

*****

"If I jump through this window it's gonna hurt."

*****

"Mean people suck, nice people swallow."

*****

"The metric system did not really catch on in the United States, unless you count the increasing popularity of the 9-millimetre bullet. - Dave Barry

*****

"Word to yo momma."

*****

"Evil reigns in the hearts of young children."

*****

"GIRL POWER

> the power to love,
> the power to think positively,
> the ability to be strong and healthy,
> the courage to say no,
> the imagination to dress as we please,
> the power not to be a tv clone,

the love to care for our friends,
the kindness to care for strangers,
the power to become anything,
the power to learn from others,
the power not to believe in magazines,
the wisdom of our mothers,
the power to be true to ourselves,
the persistence to reach our goals,
the power to be loved,
and most of all we have the power to be
AMAZING"

*****

"I wish I can do whatever I want. I wish I knew what I want."

*****

"Never regret anything; you can't change what you have done, but you can learn from it."

*****

"Expect the best but be prepared for the worst."

*****

"If you find it in your heart to care for somebody else, then you have succeeded." - Mary Angelou

*****

"An inch is a cinch a yard is hard."

*****

"When you're in jail, a good friend will be trying to bail you out. A best friend will be in the cell next to you saying, 'Damn, that was fun'." - Groucho Marx

*****

"She never gave up. My mom is my hero."
- Kimberly Ann Brand

*****

"Jump!" - Joseph Campbell

*****

"Although the world is full of suffering, it is also full of the overcoming of it." - Helen Keller

*****

"When your sad, get a friend. When your mad, stay away from them." - Janna

*****

"Never be ashamed for being human, only be ashamed for trying not to be."

*****

"From each according to his ability, to each according to his needs." - Karl Marx

*****

"May the road rise up to meet you. May the wind be always at your back. May the sunshine warm upon your face, the rain fall soft upon your fields and, until we meet again may God hold you in the palm of his hand."

*****

"Finding your mate is like installing a new floor, lay it right the first time, and you can walk on it for life."

*****

"Success comes to those who try again and again."

*****

"Everyone can sing and everyone can dance, just not everyone can sing and dance." - Nate Bradin

*****

"There are two rules to life which I live by; go with the flow and don't give a f***!"

*****

"We do not stop playing because we grow old;
we grow old because we stop playing."
- Oliver Wendell Holmes

*****

"The optimist thinks this is the best of all possible worlds. The pessimist fears it is true."
- Robert Oppenheimer

*****

"Violence is the last refuge of the incompetent."
- Isaac Asimov

*****

"I have little advice for the young teenagers of our world: May you trust in the one thing that will always be there for you; your friends. When life goes to s**t, it's all you have. Never take advantage of them, for in your darkest hour, it is all you will have."

*****

"Life is like riding a bicycle. To keep your balance you must keep moving." - Albert Einstein

*****

"Why can't all of life's problems hit us when we are 17 and know everything?"

*****

"Don't judge me without knowing me. You may hate me for jealousy."

*****

"God will never give you anything that you can't handle."

*****

"Someday someone will thank you for letting me go."

*****

"To the world you may be one person, but to one person you may be the world." - Dr Seuss

*****

"Life is like a garden, dig it!"

*****

"No, it didn't hurt when I fell from heaven, it hurt when they clipped my wings for being the devil."

*****

"And you Shall know the truth and the truth will set you free." - John 8:32

*****

"Society highly values its normal man. It educates children to lose themselves and to become absurd, and thus to be normal. Normal men have killed perhaps 100,000,000 of their fellow normal men in the last fifty years." - R.D. Laing

*****

"Never pick a fight. walk away from one, but if you have to fight, fight to win."

*****

"Sticks and stones may break my bones, but chains and whips excite me."

*****

"Smoke a smoke, not a butt, f*** a virgin not a slut."

*****

"I believe my Cupid is dead. He went to shoot the one I luv but shot himself instead."

*****

"If u could see yourself the way others do you'd wish u were as beautiful as you."

*****

"Learn from the past, live in the present, but play the game with your eyes on the future."

*****

"A baby is God's opinion that the world should go on."

*****

"If you don't have nothing nice to say then don't say nothing at all." - Chitown

*****

"Never doubt yourself. Throughout life there will be millions of people to do that for you. You do not need one more."

*****

"The enemy of your enemy is your friend."

*****

"His designs were strictly honourable, as the phrase is; that is, to rob a lady of her fortune by way of marriage." - Henry Fielding

*****

"I did not have sexual relations with that women."
- Bill Clinton

*****

"One of life's obstacles is finding out who you exactly are. However, it's not always an obstacle that we can all accomplish."

*****

"It's the piece of bread you don't check that will kill you."

*****

"I'm never alone, but I'm alone all the time." - Bush

*****

"Love and Equality are natural currents and nothing can keep them down forever."

*****

"A fact is only something you can make other people believe."

*****

"When you wake from a dream sometimes you just want to damn reality, but it's in reality that your dreams come true."

*****

"Have no fear of perfection; you'll never reach it."
- Salvador Dali

*****

"If there was no lesson to be learnt in life, there would be no life."

*****

"Not your past but your future, not your failures but your dreams, not your imperfections but your capabilities. Looking back and being proud."

*****

"Your worst enemies are your friends."

*****

"Always love and you shall be loved."

*****

"You **ck up to learn, you live to understand, you die to know."

*****

"Never tell your faith, but live it!" - Dea

*****

"Remember! God comes in many forms, but the ones who truly love him can see them."

*****

"You are only young once, make it worth remembering."

*****

"We who are truly brave will never live in fear."

*****

"If you look back into the past you cannot alter your future."

*****

"Love is a four-letter word that f***s you up."

*****

"What goes around comes around."

*****

"Peace, pot, micro-dot."

*****

"Keep on trippin!"

*****

"Friends are like money, easy to make, but hard to save." - Dea

*****

"There are only two kinds of wine, good and bad."
- Rick

*****

"How you deal with adversity and challenges will shape your life more than almost anything else."

*****

"Suicide sometimes comes from cowardness, but not always. Sometimes it prevents it, since as many people live because they are afraid to die, as die because they are afraid to live."
- Charles Caleb Colton, Lacon

*****

"Buy her a flower, and she'll think your sweet. Buy her mom a flower, and you'll sweep her off her feet."

*****

"Don't say you love someone until you know what love is."

*****

"You don't know what you've got till it's gone."

*****

"A man is not judged by who he is in life but by how he lived it."

*****

"When the tides of life turn against you and the current upsets your boat, don't waste those tears on what might have been just lie on your back and float."

*****

"Life is what u make it, not what someone u know wishes your life to be."

*****

"Worry is a thing of the past, because you worry about what has happened, worry is a thing of the future, because you worry about what will happen, but worry is never a thing of the present."

*****

"First mistake is experience, second mistake is denial, third mistake is stupidity."

*****

"That men do not learn very much from the lessons of history is the most important of all the lessons of history." - Aldous Huxley

*****

"Love is only a dirty trick played on us to achieve continuation of the species."
- William Somerset Maugham

*****

"You're not lazy you're an active stump, you're not dumb you're a smart rock."

*****

"Live the way you want, do the things you want becuz HEY you only live once."

*****

"Focus forced is lost, while focus laxed is gained." (Think of it for a while it makes sense. Would save us some money on anti-anxiety/depression in the United States if people lived by it.)

*****

"Don't wait for time, because time won't wait for you."

*****

"If you can't be with the one you love, love the one you're with."

*****

"A world without color is not worth living in."

*****

"If u luv something set it free, if it comes back 2 u then it is yours. If not, hunt it down and shoot it!"

*****

"I'm a man with the same limits of anyone of my generation. But I've never said what I didn't want to say, even if I've not always said what I wanted to say."
- Enzo Biagi

*****

"Luck is when preparation and opportunity meet."

*****

"Things are useless unless you use them."

*****

"You could shut me up, but my words will always remain." - Jordan

*****

"Truth shall set you free."

*****

"A life is touched in time and teachers do just that."

*****

"The more you sweat in practice, the less you bleed in war."

*****

"Remember, if earth didn't suck, we'd all be out in space."

*****

"The salary of the chief executive of a large corporation is not a market award for achievement. It is frequently in the nature of a warm personal gesture by the individual to himself."
- John Kenneth Galbraith

*****

"It's better to burn out than to fade away."

*****

"Peace, love, empathy." - Kurt Cobain

*****

"The eyes see what the mind can comprehend."

*****

"Everything sucks."

*****

"You may believe that you cannot succeed. That may be true, but if you don't try you will never find out."

*****

"A friend is a second self."

*****

"No husband has ever been shot while doing the dishes."

*****

"A critic is a legless man who teaches running."
- Channing Pollock

*****

"It will all be Ok in the end, if its not Ok then it's not the end."

*****

"Some love and some count the letters. the ones that love say the others fear love but then they forget to count the letters."

*****

"You are your own worst critic."

*****

"Life is a cookie. Enjoy!"

*****

"One can never see the future when reminded of the past."

*****

"If you can't duck it, ***k it!"

*****

"Great minds discuss ideas. Average minds discuss events. Small minds discuss people."

*****

"A cynic is not merely one who reads bitter lessons from the past, he is one who is prematurely disappointed in the future." - Sydney J. Harris

*****

"An ugly carpet will last forever." - Erma Bombeck

*****

"If pro is opposite of con, then what is the opposite of progress? Congress?"

*****

"Pain is just weakness leaving the body."

*****

"He still lives on."

*****

"Don't ever tell anybody anything. If you do, you start missing everybody." - J.D. Salinger

*****

"Intellectuals solve problems; geniuses prevent them."
- Albert Einstein

*****

"A Smile is the easiest way to improve your looks."

*****

"Middle age is when your age starts to show around your middle." - Bob Hope

*****

"Don't GO through life, GROW through life!"
- Eric Butterworth

*****

"I do not think that any civilization can be called complete until it has progressed from sophistication to unsophistication and made a conscious return to simplicity of thinking and living." - Lin Yutang

*****

"If the only tool you have is a hammer, you tend to see every problem as a nail." - Abraham Maslow

*****

"Now and then it's good to pause in our pursuit of happiness and just be happy." - Guillaume Apollinaire

*****

"I have always wanted to be somebody, but I see now I should have been more specific." - Lily Tomlin

*****

"The man who views the world at 50 the same as he did at 20 has wasted 30 years of his life." - Muhammad Ali

*****

"Outside of a dog, a book is a man's best friend. Inside of a dog, it's too dark to read." - Groucho Marx

*****

"Dream as if you'll live forever. Live as if you'll die today." - James Dean

*****

"It is surprising what people can do when they have to, and how little most people will do when they don't have to." - Walter Linn

*****

"To handle yourself, use your head; to handle others, use your heart." - Donald Laird

*****

"In youth we learn; in age we understand."
- Marie Ebner-Eschenbach

*****

"That the vulgar express their thoughts clearly, is far from true; and what perspicuity can be found among them proceeds not from the easiness of their language, but the shallowness of their thoughts."
- Samuel Johnson

*****

"We are the lovers, the dreamers, the creators who turn dreams in to reality. We are the fuel for

tomorrow's thinkers and the last breath for all of yesterday's glory. Acknowledge your destiny and utilize the gifts that have been given unto you. And in your darkest hour remember that it is sometimes necessary for the individual to be sacrificed in order to awaken the minds and the eyes of the masses."
- Jennifer Payne Cardamone

*****

"Even if you're on the right track, you'll get run over if you just sit there." - Arthur Godfrey

*****

"We are all caught up in an inescapable web of mutuality, tied in a single garment of destiny. Whatever affects one directly affects all indirectly."
- Martin Luther King

*****

"An infcriority complex would be a blessing, if only the right people had it." - Alan Reed

*****

"Ideals are like the stars: we never reach them, but like the mariners of the sea, we chart our course by them."
- Carl Schurz

*****

"Not only do most people accept violence if it is perpetuated by legitimate authority, they also regard

violence against certain kinds of people as inherently legitimate, no matter who commits it."
- Edgar Z. Friedenberg

*****

"Sure, there have been injuries and deaths in boxing, but none of them serious." - Alan Minter, boxer.

*****

"Forgiveness does not change the past, but it does enlarge the future." - Paul Boese

*****

"Be yourself, who else is better qualified?"
- Frank J. Giblin

*****

"Intolerance has been the curse of every age and state." - Samuel Davies

*****

"If, at first, you do succeed, try to hide your astonishment." - Los Angeles Times

*****

"logic will get you from A to B. Imagination will take you everywhere." - Albert Einstein

*****

"Some of us are becoming the men we wanted to marry." - Gloria Steinem

*****

"The good thing about democracy is just this: everyone can say their piece but there's no need to listen to them." - Enzo Biagi

*****

"It is better to die on your feet than to live on your knees." - Dolores Ibarruri

*****

"I am sick and tired of being sick and tired."
- Fannie Lou Hamer

*****

"Live every day as if it were your last, because one of these days, it will be." - Jeremy Schwartz

*****

"The tragedy of life is not that it ends so soon, but that we wait so long to begin it." - William. M. Lewis

*****

"You never know how far you can go until you try."

*****

"Anything you say I can throw it back in your face."

*****

"Challenges are what make life interesting; overcoming them is what makes life meaningful."
- Joshua J. Marine

*****

"You flee from a battle and become a Myth. You die in a war and become a Legend."

*****

"When it is dark enough, you can see the stars."

*****

"I've run a million miles and I hit the wall, I bounce back and I run some more."

*****

"Old Soldiers never die, they just fade away."

*****

"The only real mistake is the one from which we learn nothing." - John Powell

*****

"Skill is successfully walking a tightrope over Niagara Falls. Intelligence is not trying."

*****

"Love's a sensation caused by temptation; a man sticks his location in a girl's destination to increase the population of the next generation do u get my explanation, or do u need a demonstration?"

*****

"You are Miss Smith, the daughter of multi-millionaire banker Smith, aren't you? No? I beg your pardon, for a moment I thought I had fallen in love with you." - Groucho Marx

*****

"Never use a big word where a diminutive one will suffice."

*****

"Folk who don't know why America is the Land of Promise should be here during an election campaign." - Milton Berle

*****

"Living on Earth is expensive, but it does include a free trip around the sun every year."

*****

"We live in an age when pizza gets to your home before the police." - Jeff Marder

*****

"Birthdays are good for you; the more you have, the longer you live."

*****

"First you forget names, then you forget faces. Next you forget to pull your zipper up and finally, you forget to pull it down." - George Burns

*****

"Show me a man who is a good loser and I'll show you a man who is playing golf with his boss."
- Jim Murray

*****

"Inside me lives a skinny woman crying to get out. But I can usually shut her up with cookies."

*****

"As a child, a library card takes you to exotic, faraway places. When you're grown up, a credit card does it."
-Sam Ewing

*****

"When my parents finally realised that I was kidnapped, they snapped into action immediately: they rented out my room". - Woody Allen

*****

"The only way to keep your health is to eat what you don't want, drink what you don't like, and do what you'd rather not." - Mark Twain

*****

"Vegetarian - that's an old Indian word meaning lousy hunter."

*****

"The internet is a great way to get on the net."
- Bob Dole, US Congressman

*****

"A computer once beat me at chess, but it was no match for me at kick boxing." - Dennis Leary

*****

"The probability of someone watching you is proportional to the stupidity of your action."

*****

"Insanity: doing the same thing over and over again and expecting different results." - Albert Einstein

*****

"You know you are getting old when the candles cost more than the cake." - Bob Hope

*****

"I am a marvellous housekeeper. Every time I leave a man, I keep his house." - Zsa Zsa Gabor

*****

"The fact that some geniuses were laughed at does not imply that all who are laughed at are geniuses. They laughed at the Wright brothers. But they also laughed at Bozo the Clown." - Carl Sagan

*****

"There is nothing so absurd or ridiculous that has not at some time been said by some philosopher."
- Oliver Goldsmith

*****

"If your dog is fat, you aren't getting enough exercise."

*****

"If advertisers spent the same amount of money on improving their products as they do on advertising then they wouldn't have to advertise them."
- Will Rogers

*****

"The secret of life is honesty and fair dealing. If you can fake that, you got it made." - Groucho Marx

*****

"Where there is love there is life." - Mahatma Gandhi

*****

"My advice to you is get married: if you find a good wife, you'll be happy; if not, you'll become a philosopher." - Socrates

*****

"The happiest people don't necessarily have the best of everything. They just make the best of everything."

*****

"Life does not cease to be funny when people die any more than it ceases to be serious when people laugh."
- George Bernard Shaw

*****

"Reality is that which when you stop believing in it doesn't go away." - Philip K. Dick

*****

"One reason why I don't drink is because I wish to know when I am having a good time."
- Christian Herald

*****

"If you are patient in one moment of anger, you will avoid a hundred days of sorrow." - Tibetan proverb

*****

"A well-spent day brings happy sleep."
- Leonardo da Vinci

*****

"Laughter is the shortest distance between two people." - Victor Borge

*****

"It takes considerable knowledge just to realize the extent of your own ignorance." - Thomas Sowell

*****

"It is easy to be brave from a safe distance." - Aesop

*****

"Nothing is particularly hard if you divide it into small jobs." - Henry Ford

*****

"The difference between a democracy and a dictatorship is that in a democracy you vote first and take orders later; in a dictatorship you don't have to waste your time voting." - Charles Bukowski

*****

"Is sloppiness in speech caused by ignorance or apathy? I don't know and I don't care."
- William Safire

*****

"He who asks a question is a fool for five minutes; he who does not ask a question remains a fool forever."
- Chinese proverb

*****

"All men who have achieved great things have been great dreamers." - Orison Swett Marden

*****

"I hear and I forget. I see and I remember. I do and I understand." - Confucius

*****

"Few things help an individual more than to place responsibility upon him and to let him know that you trust him." - Booker T. Washington

*****

"The best way to escape from a problem is to solve it." - Alan Saporta

*****

"Ignorance is a cancer sweeping through our great society and I fear that if the remaining few of us that are untouched by this damnation do not work to save the succeeding generations then we shall all fall into the abyss." - Joshua Thomas Lunsford

*****

"Weaselling out of things is important to learn. It's what separates us from the animals; except the weasel." - Homer J Simpson

*****

"My prerogative right now is to just chill and let all the other overexposed blondes on the cover of Us Weekly be your entertainment." - Britney Spears

*****

"The price of greatness is responsibility."
- Sir Winston Churchill

*****

"Every problem has a gift for you in its hands."
- Richard Bach

*****

"You have to have Soul. But if you don't have Soul, Halibut will do." - The Muppets

*****

"Some people think it's holding on that makes one strong; sometimes it's letting go." - Sylvia Robinson

*****

"From the moment I picked up your book until I laid it down, I was convulsed with laughter. Someday I intend reading it." - Groucho Marx

*****

"Life is not the amount of breaths you take, it's the moments that take your breath away."
- Will Smith, in Hitch.

*****

"Being outside the box and not being able to shoot is like dancing with your sister." - Diego Maradona

*****

"Mankind must put an end to war, or war will put an end to mankind." - John F. Kennedy

*****

"It is one of the great truths in this world that you can never go back." - Bobo Finkelstein

*****

"The Journey of a thousand miles must begin with a single step."

*****

"Underestimation shall be the downfall of us all."
- David Beck

*****

"Peace within oneself is necessary to counteract the terror messages with which the powers-that-be try to aggravate everyone's lives." - Arturo Paoli

*****

"Burning bridges may be a bad philosophy, but I'll be damned if those fires don't look cool." - Reiko

*****

"Life is a knock down drag out brawl and if you don't keep your head up your going to get your ass kicked."
- Reiko

*****

"Life, itself is a vision, a dream. Nothing exists, but empty space and you. And you, are but a thought."

*****

"If you're not sure you can succeed, then don't waste your time." - Christa Marie Ledford

*****

"Up with miniskirts!"

*****

"For all the people out there who don't like themselves: How can someone love you if you don't love yourself?"

*****

"Love is a game which u have to play not by the rules, but by intelligence."

*****

"Two thirds of all statistics are made up."

*****

"It's true! light does travel faster than sound, someone may seem bright until they open their mouth."

*****

"Eagles may soar, but weasels don't get sucked into jet engines."

*****

"Of course, you have to go out on a limb sometimes, that's where the fruit is."

*****

"The worldwide shortage of food that threatens up to five hundred million children could be alleviated at the cost of only one day of modern warfare."
- Peter Ustinov

*****

"If you're going to tell people the truth, be funny or they'll kill you." - Billy Wilder

*****

"Utopia is on the horizon. I move two steps closer, it moves two steps further away. I walk another ten steps and the horizon runs ten steps further away. As much as I may walk, I'll never reach it. So what's the point of utopia? The point is this: to keep walking."
- Eduardo Galeano

*****

"When in doubt, overload. When in trouble retrograde."

*****

"Democracy is a pathetic belief in the collective wisdom of individual ignorance." - H.L. Mencken

*****

"I spent a lot of money on booze, birds and fast cars. The rest I just squandered." - George Best

*****

"If the Republicans will stop telling lies about the Democrats, we will stop telling the truth about them.
- Adlai E. Stevenson

*****

"A disadvantageous peace is always better than the most righteous war." - Erasmus of Rotterdam.

*****

"The best argument against democracy is a five-minute conversation with the average voter"
- Winston Churchill

*****

"If we want an end to ethnic conflict we have to invest less in war and more in the culture of peace."
- Frederico Mayor Zaragoza

*****

"The hope of becoming rich is one of the most widespread causes of poverty." - Tacitus

*****

"Whatever I don't know, I learnt at school."
- Ennio Flaiano

*****

"A shadow is lost in too much light, or too much darkness." - Moni Ovadia

*****

"A person hasn't lived unless they are remembered."

*****

"Don't allow the imposition of the liberty of speech before having the liberty of thought."
- Stanislaw Jerzy Lec

*****

"Politics is the art of seeing that people do not become interested in that which concerns them." - Paul Valéry

*****

"Military intelligence is a contradiction in terms."
- Groucho Marx

*****

"I believe that someday, we will deserve to be free of governments." - Jorge Luis Borges

*****

"Why do we kill people who have killed other people? To tell other people that killing is wrong?"
- Norman Mailer

*****

"The end may justify the means as long as there is something that justifies the end."- Leon Trotsky

*****

"A speech belongs half to the speaker and half to the listener." - Michel de Montaigne

*****

"Practice makes perfect, and nobody is perfect, so why practice?" - Billy Corgan, Smashing Pumpkins

*****

"Temptations, unlike opportunities, will always give you a second chance." - Orlando Aloysius Battista

*****

"Be the change that you wish to see in the world."
- Mahatma Gandhi

*****

"I am part of all that I have found on my road."
- Alfred Tennyson

*****

"When I grow up, I want to be a little boy."
- Joseph Heller

*****

"It just feels so weird; you mean that Mr. Aeral is dead?

Well that and my pants are full of starfish."
- The Muppets, Treasure Island

*****

"The nicest people in the world can break hearts the easiest."

*****

"God, often in his wisdom sends his angels down to walk with us. We know them best as friends."

*****

"To get where you're going, you gotta start where you are." - Steve Tollefson

*****

"A guest is like a fish, both after 3 days start to smell."

*****

"God never closes a door without opening a window first."

*****

"Cry me a river, build me bridge, and get over it."

*****

"I guess in our society, being male and an a**hole make you worthy of our time."
- 10 Things I Hate About You

*****

"The thing I'm scared of most is walking out of this room and never feeling the way I do when I'm with you." - Dirty Dancing

*****

"Sometimes it stops sometimes it flows, baby that is how love goes."

*****

"Great occasions do not make heroes or cowards; they simply unveil them to the eyes of men. Silently and imperceptibly, as we wake or sleep, we grow strong or weak; and at last some crisis shows what we have become." - Brooke Fosse Westcott

*****

"People who are wrapped up in themselves make small packages." - Benjamin Franklin

*****

"In all ages, hypocrites called priests, have put crowns on the heads of thieves, called kings."
- Robert Green Ingersoll

*****

"I will not say I have failed 1000 times; I will say that I discovered there are 1000 ways that can cause failure." - Thomas Edison

*****

"The closer to the family, the closer to the wine."

*****

"The only statistics you can trust are those you falsified yourself." - Winston Churchill

*****

"What we have in common is that we are all different from each other."

*****

"In the end, we will remember not the words of our enemies but the silence of our friends."
- Martin Luther King

*****

"We inhabit a language rather than a country."
- Emile Cioran

*****

"You don't stop laughing because you grow old. You grow old because you stop laughing."

*****

"If you're born poor it's not your mistake, but if you die poor it is your mistake." - Bill Gates

*****

"Three sentences for getting success: a) Know more than others. b) Work more than others. c) Expect less than others." - William Shakespeare

*****

"In a day when you don't come across any problems, you can be sure that you are traveling in a wrong path." - Swami Vivekananda

*****

"People who only dream only dream."

*****

"If you win, you need not explain, but if you lose you should not be there to explain." - Adolph Hitler

*****

"Don't compare yourself with anyone in this world. If you do so, you are insulting yourself." - Alan Strike

*****

"Believing everybody is dangerous; believing nobody is very dangerous." - Abraham Lincoln

*****

"Winning doesn't always mean being first. Winning means you're doing better than you've done before"
- Bonnie Blair

*****

"A person who never made a mistake never tried anything new." - Albert Einstein

*****

"No matter how hard you try, you can't control what you're like. Your friends and enemies are the ones that make you who you are."

*****

"Life's a beach, so go swimming. Or, life's a bi***, so be a bi***."

*****

"Death taxes all."

*****

"If young love is a game then I must have missed the kick-off." - Blink - 182

*****

"A smile is a crooked line that sets things straight."

*****

"If you live in a glass, don't throw stones!"

*****

"The question of whether or not computers can think is just as interesting as the question of if a submarine can swim."

*****

"Hey I need something to hold up the halo after all."
- Jake the Great

*****

"How can you trust when you've been lied, how can you dream if you've been weakened, then you can only have faith because when all hope is gone there is always faith."

*****

"I'd like to think that I didn't lose my virginity, I know where it is, I just like to think he's borrowing it for a while and maybe one day he'll give it back."

*****

"You can lead a horse to water but a pencil must be lead."

*****

"Man is the only animal that blushes - or needs to."
- Mark Twain

*****

"Being normal is the same as perfection neither exist."

*****

"We're so trendy that we can't even escape ourselves."
- Kurt Cobain

*****

"I would rather be dead than cool." - Kurt Cobain

*****

"I'm only afraid of not knowing fear." - Kurt Cobain

*****

"Kurt, you're dead but not gone!"

*****

"Marriage is the chief cause of divorce."
- Groucho Marx

*****

"A world is supported by four things; the learning of the wise, the justice of the great, the prayer of the righteous and the valor of the brave." - Frank Herbert

*****

"Follow your heart not your penis."

*****

"There are no erasers big enough to erase the mistakes made in life."

*****

"Before you insult someone you should walk a mile in their shoes, that way when you insult them, you are a mile away and have their shoes."

*****

"Win my heart with words, and soul, not flowers."

*****

"How many times must my heart bleed, until it is melted?"

*****

"Don't get mad, don't get even, don't feel anger, don't push others, don't listen to others. Think about it!"

*****

"When anger fails, try love."

*****

"If you want something, go get it!"

*****

"Nothing is gained without effort. Even that which appears to have been gained without effort, soon depart from us because of our lack thereof. We must first conduct business in order to create pleasure. There is no other way."

*****

"If all the search engines on my computer cannot find God then how can I ask him questions?"

*****

"Never be what someone else is, just so you can get credit from them and others. Always be what you are, and what you are is what you choose to be. Choose your own destiny. Don't let anyone, even if God himself, choose your destiny for you, because then you are them, because you are what they choose for you to be."

*****

"You can't please everyone, so you, got to please yourself." - Ricky Nelson

*****

"Pain is nothing but fear leaving your body."

*****

"A man who sleeps on the floor did not fall off the bed." - Roger

*****

"Second Place is the first loser."

*****

"Fear no one, trust no one, and live. Fear everyone, trust everyone, and die."

*****

"The very purpose of existence is to reconcile the glowing opinion we hold of ourselves with the appalling things that other people think about us." - Quentin Crisp

*****

"If the first fifteen days of the month are dark, the other fifteen will be bright."

*****

"Have a Bob day!"

*****

"Look for the ridiculous in everything and you will find it." - Jules Renard

*****

"If he really did love me, then why did he leave?"

*****

"I have one day to live. Should I go shopping or should I spend it with the guy I fell in love with? Neither, they cost me way too much in the past."

*****

"There's always room at the top."

*****

"If you sprinkle when u tinkle, please be neat and wipe the seat."

*****

"A good traveller has no fixed plans and is not intent on arriving." - Lao Tzu (570-490 BC)

*****

"I will wash my brain in the splendid breeze, I will lay my cheek to the northern sun, I will drink the breath of the mossy trees, and the clouds shall meet me one by one. I will fling the scholar's pen aside, and grasp once more the bronco's reign, till the rain is snow and the seed is grain. The way is long and cold and lone, but I go. It leads where pines forever moan, they're weight of snow, yet I go. There are voices in the wind that call, there are hands that beckon to the plain."
- Hamlin Garland

*****

"The woodman's echoing stroke, the holy silence of the forest broke; now first was heard the crash of falling trees, yielding to other power than howling breeze; and now the first time did the furrow tear the virgin Earth, and lay her bosom bare."
- James Fenimore Cooper

*****

"The road to truth is long and lined the entire way with annoying bast**ds." - Alexander Jablokov

*****

"In New Mexico he always awoke a young man. He had noticed that this particular quality in the air of new countries vanished after they were tamed by man and made to bear harvests. That only on the bright edges of the world, on the great grass plains or the sagebrush desert. Something soft and wild and fee; something that whispered to the ear on the pillow, lightened the heart, softly, softly picked the lock, slid the bolts, and released the prisoned spirit of man into the wind, into the blue and gold, into the morning, into the morning." - Willa Cather

*****

"If you believe yourself to be a winner eventually you will become one. Until then, keep practicing!"

*****

"Men stumble over the truth from time to time, but most pick themselves up and hurry off as if nothing happened." - Winston Churchill

*****

"He is one of those people who would be enormously improved by death." - H.H. Munro

*****

"Mr. Rabbit says the moment of realization is worth a thousand prayers." - Natural Born Killers

*****

"To be or not to be will always be the question, I am what I am will always be the answer." - Anna

*****

"Wishes come true, not free." - Into the Woods

*****

"We are all so strong when nothings wrong and the world is at your feet, but how small we are when our love is far away, and all I need is you." - K´s Choice

*****

"To know you is to hate you, so loving you must be like suicide." - Green Day

*****

"Show me a sane person and I'll cure him."
- Karl Jung

*****

"Gravity always wins." - Radiohead

*****

"Trying to keep the pain, kill the dead, and burn the rain."

*****

"Be Calm, gives you time for the coolest reaction."

*****

"Once you find your self esteem, then you're forever free to dream." - Shania Twain

*****

"Life moves pretty fast if you don't stop and take a look around for a while you could miss it."

*****

"If you settle for everything, you'll get nothing."

*****

"You never remember the day, only the moment, so make every moment count."

*****

"Life is like a di**, when it gets hard... f*** it!"

*****

"You only live once, but if you do it right, once is enough." - Mae West

*****

"Time kills everything." - Mark Ziaian

*****

"He travels fastest who travels alone."
- Rudyard Kipling

*****

"Don't walk in front of me, I may not follow. Don't walk behind me, I may not lead. Walk beside me, just be my friend." - Albert Camus

*****

"Let us enrich ourselves with our mutual differences."
- Paul Valéry

*****

"They say there's a heaven for those who will wait. Some say it's better, but I say it ain't. I'd rather laugh with the sinners than cry with the saints. Sinners are much more fun. And only the good die young."
- Billy Joel

*****

"You can learn a lot from people who view the world differently than you do." - Anthony J. D'Angelo

*****

"If you tell the truth, you don't have to remember anything." - Mark Twain

*****

"A day without sunshine is like, you know, night."
- Steve Martin

*****

"A woman is like a teabag; you never know how strong it is until it's in hot water." - Eleanor Roosevelt

*****

"A friend is someone who knows everything about you and still loves you." - Elbert Hubbard

*****

"Live as if you will die tomorrow. Learn as if you will live forever." - Mahatma Gandhi

*****

"If you want to know what a man's like, take a good look at how he treats his inferiors, not his equals."
- J.K Rowling (Harry Potter and the Goblet of Fire)

*****

"If you live your life in regret, you'll end up regretting it." - Mark Ziaian

*****

"Love all, trust a few, do wrong to none."
- William Shakespeare (All's Well That Ends Well)

*****

INDEX

www.ingramcontent.com/pod-product-compliance
Lightning Source LLC
Chambersburg PA
CBHW071903020426